ADVANCE PRAISE

"*Kaleidoscope* speaks to the fundamental values that drive innovative service: trust, authenticity, and genuine care. Weaving together colorful anecdotes and firsthand experiences from across disparate industries, Chip reveals a common truth: At the heart of innovative service lives true passion—the key to creating memorable experiences and building customer loyalty."

> **—J. Allen Smith, president and CEO, Four Seasons Hotels and Resorts**

"Chip Bell articulates perfectly some of the fundamental truths of creating loyal customers that few people have been able to put into words so clearly. His passion for exceeding customer expectations is contagious . . . it's hard to walk away from this book without feeling inspired."

> **—Scott Scherr, CEO, president, and founder of Ultimate Software**

"*Kaleidoscope* provides a stunning virtual lens through which to view Chip Bell's stories and perspectives, which light unique pathways to delivering innovative service that makes customer experiences special. What a fantastic way to inspire me and my colleagues at WestRock to enchant our customers every day."

> **—Steve Voorhees, CEO, WestRock**

"Chip Bell has done it again! His powerful message strongly reflected in *Kaleidoscope* inspired all our general managers and company leaders to always be here for our guests and team members."

> **—Keith A. Cline, president and CEO, La Quinta Inns and Suites**

"Like a second wind allows a runner to go farther than they thought they could, Chip's concepts allowed Scooter's Coffee to think deeper and more specifically about how we raise our customer experience past the usual platitudes. 'Great' is everywhere . . . 'Amazing,' not so much. Chip has an incredible way of making what should be obvious, obvious and easy to understand."

—Don Eckles, cofounder, Scooter's Coffee

"No one knows more about practical and profitable customer service than Chip Bell. He proves it yet again in this innovative and substantive book that will tickle your imagination, inspire your thinking, and enhance your business. Highly recommended."

—Nido R. Qubein, president, High Point University ,
chairman, Great Harvest Company

"*Kaleidoscope* is a powerful wake-up call to be always noble in how we serve others. It offers a pragmatic blueprint for providing customers a value-unique experience that triggers advocacy, not just retention."

—Marshall Goldsmith, author of *New York Times* bestselling books
Triggers, Mojo,* and *What Got You Here Won't Get You There

"Chip Bell's newest book continues a tradition of mixing home-style morals and straight talk with smart, helpful marketing advice. Full of common sense and powerful business lessons, *Kaleidoscope* is a book every marketer should read."

—Don Peppers, founding partner, Peppers and Rogers Group, author of *Customer Experience: What, How, and Why Now* and *The One to One Future*

"With *Kaleidoscope*, Chip has created his own kaleidoscope of service proverbs that make you say, 'Aha!' and service parables that are stories you will long remember. This is a gem of a book that should be read by every professional involved in serving others. (And isn't that all of us?)"

—Matt Michel, CEO, The Service Roundtable

"*Kaleidoscope* is a powerful guide to how a company grows—by being of service to others. It gives you that elusive blueprint for providing customers a valuable experience that earns passionate advocates who grow your business for you."

—Jeanne Bliss, author of *Chief Customer Officer 2.0*

"Chip Bell has an enviable way of taking challenging and often daunting topics like customer loyalty and breaking them down into immediately actionable components. Rich with stories, insights, and tools, *Kaleidoscope* is a must-have resource for anyone who wants to bring to life a colorful 'kaleidoscope' of special and memorable connections with those they serve. Thanks, Chip, for an enchanting resource!"

—**Joseph Michelli, *New York Times* #1 bestselling author of books like *Driven to Delight: Delivering World-Class Customer Experience the Mercedes-Benz Way* and *The Starbucks Experience***

"Value–added, extraordinary, memorable service is much more than *what* we do, it is the heart, spirit, and soul we put *into* what we do that makes the difference. Customers know when they experience 'spirit led' customer service! And you will recognize it when you read these pages."

—**Sharon Allred Decker, COO, Tryon Equestrian Partners, Carolinas' Operations, former North Carolina Secretary of Commerce**

"Chip always hits the nail on the head. He is the one striking at the root, not hacking at the leaves of service excellence. It's nice to see someone address the compassion side of service since 'charity never fails'"

—**Ken Shelton, CEO, Executive Excellence, LLC and former editor and publisher of *Leadership Excellence* and *Sales and Service Excellence***

KALEIDSCOPE

DELIVERING INNOVATIVE SERVICE THAT SPARKLES

CHIP R. BELL

GREENLEAF
BOOK GROUP PRESS

Published by Greenleaf Book Group Press
Austin, Texas
www.gbgpress.com

Distributed by Greenleaf Book Group

For ordering information or special discounts for bulk purchases, please contact Greenleaf Book Group
at PO Box 91869, Austin, TX 78709, 512.891.6100.

Design and composition by Greenleaf Book Group and Kim Lance
Cover design by Greenleaf Book Group and Kim Lance
Image Credits Cover: ©Thinkstock/iStock Collection/bagiuiani (lightbulb), ©Shutterstock/flowersmile (kaleidoscope pattern)
Image Credits Interior (in order of appearance): ©Thinkstock/iStock Collection/LunaticLu; Excerpt and photograph from
Walk The Line, written by Gill Dennis and James Mangold. ©2005 All Rights Reserved. Courtesy of Twentieth Century Fox;
Quote by Erin Swanson, From "The Abilene Daradox" by Jerry Harvey. Courtesy of Wiley. ©Thinkstock/iStock Collection/
sanyal, ©Thinkstock/iStock Collection/hakkiarslan, ©Thinkstock/iStock Collection/Jevtic, ©Thinkstock/iStock Collection/
efesenko, Photo and QR code courtesy of westjet; ©Thinkstock/iStock Collection/f9photos, ©Thinkstock/iStock Collection/
ipopba, Shutterstock/garmoncheg, Thinkstock/Stockbyte Collection/open sign, Shutterstock/flowersmile, Photo of Jerry Lee
Lewis.©Getty.

Cataloging-in-Publication data is available.

Print ISBN: 978-1-62634-394-8

eBook ISBN: 978-1-62634-395-5

Part of the Tree Neutral® program, which offsets the number of trees consumed in the production and printing
of this book by taking proactive steps, such as planting trees in direct proportion to the number of trees used:
www.treeneutral.com

TreeNeutral

Printed in China on acid-free paper

17 18 19 20 21 22   10 9 8 7 6 5 4 3 2 1

First Edition

CONTENTS

THE TRAILER

INSIDE THE KALEIDOSCOPE

Johnny Cash has always been a hero of mine. *Walk the Line* is a box office hit movie that depicts highlights from Johnny's life based on his biography *Man in Black*.

One of the most powerful scenes in Gill Dennis's screenplay depicts J. R. (Johnny) Cash's audition at Sun Records in Memphis, Tennessee, with Sam Phillips (the legendary producer who discovered Elvis Presley) Roy

Orbison, Carl Perkins, Jerry Lee Lewis, and B. B. King. Accompanied by his backup singers, Marshall Grant and Luther Perkins, Cash begins to sing a then-popular gospel song. Halfway through it, Phillips stops him and questions his belief in what he's singing.

Here is the actual portion of screenplay used for the movie:

J. R. Cash: You sayin' I don't believe in God?

Marshall Grant: (quietly) J. R. . . . come on, let's go.

J. R. Cash: No, I want to understand. I mean . . . we come down here, we play for a minute, and he tells me I don't believe in God.

Phillips: You know exactly what I'm tellin' you. We've already heard that song . . . a hundred times. Just like that. Just like how you sang it.

J. R. Cash: Well, you didn't let us bring it home.

Sam Phillips's confrontational response was a major turning point in Johnny's life. Without it, we perhaps never would have received the gift of music that Johnny Cash created. His many number one hit songs landed him in the Rock and Roll Hall of Fame, the Country Music Hall of Fame, and the Gospel Music Hall of Fame. But back to the movie . . .

Phillips: (chuckling) Bring it . . . Bring it home? All right, let's "bring it home." If you was hit by a truck, and you was lyin' out in that gutter dyin', and you had time to sing one song—huh?— one song people would remember before you're dirt, one song that would let . . . God . . . know what you felt about your time here on earth, one song that would sum you up, you tellin' me that's the song you'd sing? That same Jimmy Davis tune we hear on the radio all day? About your 'peace within' and how it's real and how you're gonna shout it? Or would you sing somethin' different? Somethin' real? Somethin' you felt? Cause I'm tellin' you right now, that's the kinda song people want to hear. That's the kinda song . . . that truly saves people. It ain't got nothin' to do with believin' in God, Mister Cash. It has to do with believin' in yourself.

I hope you see the movie, if just for that one great scene! But even if you don't, I hope you think about the call to action issued by Sam Phillips. Johnny Cash was a singer, a deliverer of music. What if the story line had been about a service provider . . . a deliverer of value to customers? What if it was your story and a Sam Phillips was goading you about whether you truly believed in the service you were delivering?

Service can be a perfunctory act delivered with routine banter and going-through-the-motions energy. It can be the same service we get pretty much everywhere, every day. Or, it can be something different . . . something that sums you up. It can be done so it is clear that it has meaning and is delivered from your deepest self. It can be like "Folsom Prison Blues," a song that came from the core of Johnny Cash in a way that caused Sam Phillips to recognize Cash had a truly special talent. To paraphrase Sam Phillips, that's the kind of service people want to receive. That's the kind of service that truly touches people.

This book is about innovative service, not just good customer service. Good service leaves customers satisfied; innovative service makes them swoon and become zealous advocates for your business. Innovative service comes from your core; it evokes an experience of genuineness, a sense that its source is deep, not superficial.

Innovative service is more than value-added service—taking what customers expect and adding more into it. Innovative service is value-unique—it is about delivering an experience that is surprisingly ingenious. It is like the sprinkles on an already excellent cupcake. In other words, the service experience that touches customers' hearts, not just their funny bones or happy genes, is innovative service with character and depth; service from *your* heart.

It's about more than service put together with over-the-top imagination; it's about creating the kind of experience that profoundly touches the soul of customers, leaving them forever changed by the encounter. "We live in a changing world," wrote Chick-fil-A founder S. Truett Cathy, "But we need to be reminded that the important things have not changed. . . ." This book is dedicated to being that kind of gut-checking reminder.

Kaleidoscope: Delivering Innovative Service That Sparkles is the third book in a series on innovative service—it follows *The 9½ Principles of Innovative Service* (Simple Truths, 2012) and *Sprinkles: Creating Awesome Experiences Through Innovative Service* (Greenleaf Book Group, 2014).

This latest book opens by comparing innovative service to a kaleidoscope. Like great innovative service, kaleidoscopes provide wonderful amusement. Rotating the cylinder to deliver new expressions of radiance is guaranteed to generate oohs and ahs. But the colorful pieces of glass or gems inside the

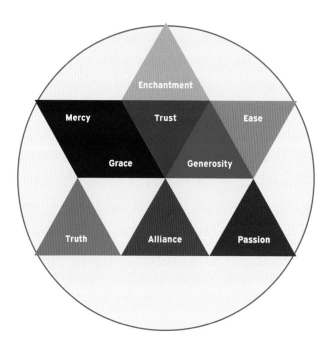

working end of the kaleidoscope never change. They are the core character of the kaleidoscope's artistic expression.

This book is about the different shades of colored glass inside the "kaleido-scope" of value-unique service; each chapter will reveal a different shade of its charisma and depth. The book also gives you an idea about what is needed to bring innovative service to life. The mechanisms that make actual kaleidoscopes work include a three-sided mirror and reflections. Innovative service requires reflecting on what is important to your customers (an "outside in" perspective), but the source of innovative service comes from within you. This is a "looking in the mirror" book (with an "inside out" viewpoint).

The cylinder part of the kaleidoscope that is rotated to make the colored glass move into a unique pattern is called an *animator*. Sprinkled throughout this book is a collection of animators—fifty action items to turn philosophy into practice and resolve into results. Remember, service with sprinkles can delight customers yet can also seem purely whimsical, merely a means to provide a temporary thrill. But service from the heart is like Phillips's advice to Cash: It shows that something novel can also be something that is profound.

We *are* what we serve to others. It is our signature that sums us up each time a customer is on the receiving end of our efforts. And, your customers remember *how* you served long after they have forgotten *what* you served! How can you deliver service in a fashion that says, "This is me, and it is my very best gift to you"?

ENCHANTMENT

ADD A LITTLE SPARKLE

"We wait, starving for moments of high magic
to inspire us, but life is full of common enchantment
waiting for our alchemists eyes to notice."

—JACOB NORDBY

The beautiful Fairmont Pacific Rim hotel on the waterfront in downtown Vancouver, British Columbia, is truly enchanting. When I stayed there, my guest room had a spectacular panoramic, twenty-first floor view of the Salish Sea. But

the best feature was displayed on the high-tech, industrial-strength work desk—a circular box of pick-up sticks, an antique slinky in its original box, and a colorful kaleidoscope!

The ultramodern furnishings bathed in an abundance of chrome, glass, and push-button everything were cheerfully contrasted with the simple, colorful toys of yesteryear. This unique blend was meant to make you pause, reflect, and feel like the room had given you a great big "welcome home" hug. The kaleidoscope grabbed my attention and held on tightly. What if the features of a kaleidoscope were embedded in experiences you create for those you serve?

Kaleidoscopes are addictive. They make you privately ooh and ah as you turn the animator and behold the patterns of colorful glass that charm you. The view can be as special as a grandchild's hug, as exciting as new puppy, and as awe-inspiring as a double rainbow. Innovative service has the same emotional influence and poignant hold. It creates a chain reaction, a tugging at our heart that triggers us to tug on our wallet.

Kaleidoscopes also have the attributes of the kind of experiences we all desire—as customers, employees, and colleagues. Notice how we all like good service, but only boast, shout, or tweet about experiences that are unique and produce an emotional connection. *Good* is the key to customer retention, but *unique* is the secret to customer advocacy. Master kaleidoscope experiences and dispense them to those you serve, and you will lasso their hearts.

Customers Care When They Share

I was enjoying a three-day stay at a Courtyard by Marriott hotel in San Antonio, Texas. Shortly after lunch on my second day, the hotel manager placed a flip chart with a hand-printed sign in the lobby. "Dear guests: We need your help. The aunt of one of our housekeepers has passed away and today is the funeral.

This was an important person in this housekeeper's life; we all felt we should be at the funeral. Consequently, there will only be one employee on site . . . at the front desk . . . between 2 and 3:30 p.m. We ask your patience and understanding. Thanks, the manager!"

Courtyard customers immediately shifted into a mode of helping each other. Guests served other guests coffee in the lobby bistro. One guest said, "Why don't I be the greeter like at Walmart?" Guests welcomed arriving guests and personally explained what was on the lobby sign. Even the next day as I was checking out, guests were still talking about how fun it was when "*We* ran the hotel!" Sometimes the most wonderful words customers can hear you say are, "I need your help." People will care when they share.

Kaleidoscopes function differently from their utilitarian cousins—binoculars, telescopes, and microscopes. Once you adjust these other devices to suit your vision, you just stare through them, much like viewing a photo. Kaleidoscopes invite you to alter the cavalcade of color and design simply by rotating the animator. The more you rotate, the higher the candlepower on your grin. And just when you think you have seen the pinnacle of glass-mosaic artwork, another image tops the one before.

Enchanting Equals Enduring

Here is your service quiz! You own a fine-dining restaurant in . . . let's say in New Orleans. You have a wonderful dessert menu customers rave about. But you notice that many patrons only order coffee since they are too stuffed to eat dessert. You do not want to make your entrée servings smaller—generosity is one of your brand distinctions. But you would love to find an ingenious way to leave guests more thrilled than a good cup of coffee is likely to ensure.

A common practice of upscale restaurants is to provide petit fours or *mignardises* (small pastries) "compliments of the chef." That's not good enough for the fabulous Restaurant R'evolution in the Royal Sonesta New Orleans hotel in the French Quarter. There, the waiter brings out a red Peruvian jewelry box with little drawers filled with mini truffles, tiny shortbreads, baby peanut butter biscotti, miniscule decorative chocolates, and such. The creation of executive pastry chef Erin Swanson (now the executive sous chef at the Pontchartrain Hotel nearby), it is the enchanting finale about which customers tell compelling stories.

When I interviewed Chef Erin about how she came up with the idea of a jewelry box for the unique presentation of her tiny desserts, she went straight to reconceiving the definition of dessert. "I always enjoyed making miniature colorful desserts. And I have always thought of them as little jewels. So, where do you put jewels?"

Enchanting, innovative service, like the image created inside the kaleidoscope, is handcrafted and intended to make recipients swoon, sigh, and giggle. It is the waitress in a Manhattan diner putting her flower arrangement from her wedding anniversary the day before on your table; the auto dealership that puts a rose on the dash of a customer's car after she has had it serviced; or the Disney World housekeeper who tucks stuffed toys into bed while the hotel room's guests are away in the theme park, making it appear as if the toys had magically come alive.

One of the most intriguing features of a kaleidoscope is that you never see the same colorful arrangement twice. This keeps us hooked and delighted. And it is an invitation to all service providers to constantly up their game. The good news is that, while there may be a limit to value-added generosity, there is no limit to value-unique ingenuity!

Examine your customers' experiences as if you were an "experience auditor" from Cirque du Soleil, Disney World, or Bass Pro Shops! What would Lady Gaga do to amaze? What would Stephen Spielberg do to enthrall? Ask a spunky eight-year-old to suggest ways to enchant. How could you add a little simple magic? What would balloons, chocolate coins, or funny or inspiring one-liners on a note do to make your customers' experiences more magical? Start every day with an "It's showtime!" attitude, and then give your customers the time of their lives. Take a page from the Fairmont Pacific Rim and add a touch of enchantment to the features of the service you deliver!

"Enchantment transforms situations
and relationships. It converts hostility into civility.
It reshapes civility into affinity.
It changes skeptics and cynics into believers."

—**GUY KAWASAKI**, author of *Enchantment*

Animators for Enchantment

A kaleidoscope, like innovative service, creates the experience of being under a magical spell. They both charm as much as they entertain—appeal as much as they intrigue. A kaleidoscope's alluring display of color and shape seems charismatic and mystical, like the simple surprise of service with ingenuity.

- Recall what you love about opening a Cracker Jack box and answer this question: What could be your monetarily inexpensive but emotionally priceless "free prize inside" your customer's experience?

- What is the color of your customers' experiences? Black and white or Technicolor? If they were inside a kaleidoscope, how would your service experiences appear to your customers? How can you make them enchanting?

- Delight is in the eye of the customer. Find out what specific features of service would elevate your customers' delight and loyalty. Ask them this: "For you to describe our customer experience to someone as awesome or uniquely delightful, what would have happened?"

- Conduct a sense audit. What could your service experience smell like, sound like, feel like, look like, taste like if you wanted to truly excite your customers in a fashion that sticks in their memory?

- Service that truly "saves" people starts with an obvious and genuine desire to serve. If your customers gave you a grade on your authentic eagerness to serve, what grade would they give you? What could you do to get an A+?

2

GRACE

HONOR YOUR CUSTOMER

"I do not at all understand the mystery of grace
—only that it meets us where we are
but does not leave us where it found us."

—ANNE LAMOTT

Howard Perdue was the owner, manager, and spiritual leader of the Ford Tractor dealership in McRae, Georgia, during the fifties and sixties. In that era, about 185 percent of the population—practically every man, woman, child, dog, and mule—was involved in the overtime occupation of worrying about soybean prices and praying for rain. Since no one could do much serious farming without a tractor and the proper plows, Mr. Perdue was the center of the universe. He was also my mother's brother.

The Perdue-farmer relationship was a special one. Few farmers started the planting season with enough money to fund all their farm equipment needs. They typically bet—along with Howard—on the success of their harvest. Their new combine or fertilizer spreader was bought on credit and a promise to pay "when I make my crop." Frequently, farmers literally "bet the farm" when an

unexpected equipment failure led to an unforeseen expense. But the risk was not only on the customer's side; if the farmer could not harvest their crops, Howard lost as well.

I once overheard a troubled farmer pleading his cash shortage problem to Carl Vardaman, who ran the parts counter. "I'm sure Mr. Howard will understand your situation," Carl assured him. I watched from behind the counter as Howard emerged from the garage, wiping engine grease from his hands. The farmer and Howard greeted each other without shaking hands—farmers generally only shook hands with the preacher when leaving the church. "How's Mary?" Howard asked, attempting to alter the straight lines on the farmer's downcast face.

I didn't hear their conversation—they went behind closed doors. But when they emerged, Howard announced to Carl that Mr. Garrison would be getting a new carburetor. It was coded communication—a signal from Howard to Carl that credit had been extended, boundaries expanded, and trust restored. The farmer left with his head held high. Grace performs marvelous feats.

Grace is also a word with a heavy load. Some words are simple, with a singular direct meaning. Not *grace*. It can mean simple elegance—as in, a sense of class and polish. We use it when we describe the effortless movement of a superb athlete or the easy graciousness of a host. Grace can mean honoring the presence of someone—"You grace us with your company"—and grace can shoulder its biggest payload in the religious definition of "unmerited or unconditional favor or love."

Graceful service is an assertion, not a response. It is an attitude, not a tactic. We get a glimpse when we witness a random act of kindness. But service full of grace is not random; it is perpetual. To riff on a line from Jack Nicholson in the movie *As Good as It Gets*, it makes a customer want to be a better person. Like some mysterious alchemy, when compassion meets caustic, all the acidity disappears. Grace not only tames hostility, it enriches the ordinary and elevates "I got my money's worth" to "I have a story to tell."

Always Count on Goodness

Archeologists excavating the pyramids discovered an unexpected treasure— wheat seeds that dated back to around 2,500 BC. As in the tradition of antiquity, the seeds were there for the dead pharaohs to eat if they got hungry. The find would enable scientists to determine what variety of wheat was in use in the ancient world and could be invaluable for launching new strains of wheat. Out of curiosity, the scientists planted the 4,500-year-old wheat seeds in fertile soil, and an amazing thing happened. They grew!

The seed story has always amazed me. How could seeds that ancient still grow? Then, a friend pointed out that the moral of the story might not be in the seeds, but rather in the fertile soil. "Every living thing on the planet," he advised me, "has the capacity to do remarkable things if placed in fertile soil." Innovative service starts with the assumption of the goodness of customers. And such a belief can ignite a self-fulfilling prophecy. Customers treated with goodness assume the behavior and attitude of goodness.

The assumption of goodness is manifested as sincere respect. When I was a kid, I used to accompany my grandfather to town in his pickup truck to buy a few bags of feed for his cows. To and from the feed store we talked about stuff like two old friends, not like an elder and a kid talking. And he always introduced me as Mr. Chip to the people we encountered. If the sales person at the feed store asked him how many bags he wanted loaded, he would point toward me and declare, "Mr. Chip can tell you." As a ten-year-old, I felt very grown up. It is that same type of declaration, respect, and affirmation that provides fertile soil for growing a customer relationship.

How would an assumption of goodness have changed the outcome in that famous scene in *Pretty Woman* when Vivian Ward was treated with arrogance and disdain? What would have happened if Howard Perdue had played stern banker instead of benevolent neighbor with his neighbor in need? Instead of watching rejection at Howard's tractor store, I saw sincere respect, and rather than judgment, I witnessed grace. And the payoff was plain to see when Howard showered all three definitions of grace upon his grateful customer.

Serve with Bold Altruism

Everyone, regardless of faith or theology, knows the story of the Good Samaritan. The parable is about a man who stops to give aid to someone who hates him. The man who needs help is a robbery victim and Jewish; at the time, Samaritans were considered by many to be an inferior people whom they despised. Think of the view as similar to the one that bigoted whites in the Deep South held of Afri-

can-Americans in the early 1950s.

But there is an unfamiliar part of this all-familiar story. Before stopping to help his "neighbor," the Samaritan had walked from Jericho to Jerusalem, thirty miles uphill on challenging, rocky terrain populated by thieves. The route was called *The Way of Death*. Despite the exhaustion and anxiety from his journey, he stops to help his enemy, transports him to a nearby inn, and covers all his costs. He could have said, "I am too tired," "I'll be rejected," or "This is too hard." Instead, he invests in the situation in a way that makes all the difference. It is more than a gift; it is a bold and conscious sacrifice.

Tom's Shoes donates a pair of shoes to a child in need for each pair a customer purchases from the company. Scooter's Coffee sources 100 percent of their coffee beans from shade tree plantations. Customers know that each cup they drink saves two square yards of rainforest in Latin America. When Houston based Hilcorp Energy made a challenging corporate goal, all 1,380 employees, regardless of position, got a performance bonus—$100,000 each. Graceful service takes more than routine effort or everyday contribution: it is an abundance of spirit; it is contribution beyond what is reasonable; it is altruistic.

Be the giver you hope your customers become. Show your most focused, treasure-hunting curiosity. Be slow to blame, quick to affirm, and the very best at celebrating your customers. Always do what you say you will do. If you can't, renegotiate early. Check all greed at the door. The world of work works when there is a deep-rooted connection to the conscience rather than a myopic focus on the competition. In the words of Tara Hunt in her classic book *The Whuffie Factor*, marketplace influence comes through "being nice, being networked, and being notable. There is no room for bullies or lots of money. Money may buy you an audience, but it will not guarantee influence."

We live in an era of cynicism. Customers today are on guard, half expecting a scam, rip-off, or unfair treatment. They witness hidden fees, nickel-and-diming practices, and greed-driven pricing. The venom often found on customer review sites reflects pent-up scorn from a collection of disappointments, not just a single incident. This makes graceful service a powerful remedy to indifference and irritation. It begins with acting like every day is your customer's birthday. You can start igniting grace with a simple, "I am here to serve and daringly make a difference in your life."

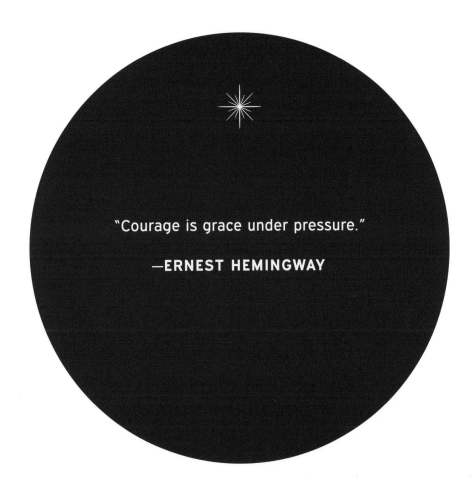

"Courage is grace under pressure."

—ERNEST HEMINGWAY

Animators for Grace

"Is there a light inside it?" my granddaughter asked while looking through the business end of my antique kaleidoscope. "No," I said. "The light comes from the outside and shines through this end." I could see the wheels of insight turning in her head. "So, it's like being really nice to people you don't even know." She is clearly developing the wisdom to animate her relationship with grace!

- Respect is not what you believe; it is what you show. Use *sir* and *ma'am* to people you do not normally address in that manner. Take actions that would get you the Ms. or Mr. Great Manners award!

- Avoid giving any one-word answers to your customers' questions.

- Be a proactive guardian of your customers' dignity. Stand up for their significance. Never let anyone hear you bad-mouth a customer.

- Be the best example of integrity your customer has ever seen by always doing what is right and not being fixated on what is allowed.

- Graceful service that is profound is the type that assumes innocence, even with a history of the opposite. Judgment fuels defensiveness, for you and your customer.

Over 45 million people have watched this seriously sparkly expression of grace. Point your QR Reader to the left and watch it again. If you are new to Quick Response (QR) codes, turn to page 108 for a quick explanation.

3

TRUST

KEEP YOUR COVENANTS

"A relationship with no trust is like a cell phone with
no service; all you can do is play games."

—UNKNOWN

The coolest birthday present I ever received was a gift from my wife a number of years ago; it was a white 1962 Mercedes-Benz 220 sedan reasonably well restored. The classy antique car, with its deep fenders and leather seats, turned out to be a real lemon. That's about all I remember about the car. But I remember a lot about

Brothers Auto Service near Charlotte, North Carolina, where we were living at the time. Brothers was where my elegant birthday present was frequently nursed back to health during the two years I tried to depend on it.

The two owners, Nicky and Joe, believed all customers were simply "good neighbors with car problems." Their prices were fair, their workmanship superb, their hours convenient, but the same could be said of most of their competitors, including the service department of a major Mercedes dealership that

was less than a mile away! It's their "in customers we trust" philosophy that has kept Brothers in business since 1982.

Long before the era of loaner cars, Nicky and Joe would often say, "We'll need about two hours to fix your car, so if you have errands you need to run, just take my car." Nicky drove a top-of-the-line Mercedes; Joe drove a BMW. Their courageous trust in their customers was reciprocated. Customers gave Nicky or Joe complete license to replace a part or perform an unexpected repair without calling or asking for permission. And, "repaired such and such, no charge" appeared on many of their repair orders. The relationship was a pure partnership laced with trust.

The anatomy of trust reveals its irrational, emotional, and perceptual nature. We trust lots of medical personnel whose resumes we never check. We trust the food we eat in a restaurant without a visit to their kitchen. "Real trust," wrote Seth Godin, "doesn't always come from divulging, from providing more transparency, but from the actions that people take (or that we think they take) before our eyes. It comes from people who show up before they have to, who help us when they think no one is watching."[1] Trust building is homegrown (from the heart) and handmade (actions speak louder than words).

Make Promise Keeping Your Signature

Johnny Cash began every concert with the words, "Hi, I'm Johnny Cash." It was a way of signaling to his audience that everything to follow was to be a reflection of *who* he was, not just *what* he did. It was the signature of his soul! Service always has the signature of someone on it. Even if customers are not always certain whose name is hardwired into the service source code, a person's name is there somewhere.

My dad taught me as a boy to be a person whose word was his bond and promise keeping was his signature. We live our lives on promises. From the time a child can grasp the concept of "cross my heart and hope to die," there is a forever awareness that anxiety can be only reduced through proof of trust while waiting for a promise to be kept. From "Scout's honor" to "I do" to "the whole truth and nothing but the truth," we seek cues that allay our worries. Lifeguards, the bus schedule, and the spotlessness of a hospital room are all obvious artifacts of promises waiting to be kept.

Service begins with a promise made or implied. Promises sound like, "We'll be landing on time," "It will be ready by noon," or "Your order will be right out." We sense its subtle power when the hotel finds our reservation, the newspaper is on the front porch, or the bank statement is accurate. Even the brand symbol itself can connote trustworthiness from the quality of the coffee to the charm of a magical character. Trust is the emotion that propels customers to the other side of the gap between promise and proof.

Honor Your Covenant

Honor and trust are the lifeblood of repeat business. To serve well is to enter into a covenant with a customer that guarantees worth will be exchanged for worth and in a way that keeps central the customers' best interests. When customers suspect any hint of disrespect or deceit—a deficit of honor—the odds of their walking through that organization's doors again fall precipitously.

Honor is the soul of the service covenant. We rely on it to govern fair and proper practice. Service interactions aren't regulated by formal contracts that bind the server and the served to virtuous behaviors—customers simply assume they'll be treated in a respectful, ethical, and civil manner. When they aren't, cracks begin to form in their repurchase intentions. Should customers experience further disrespectful or dishonest behavior, those fissures grow into fault lines that rupture and send them drifting away to the competition. Those who serve customers with honor act as "trustodians," constantly guarding the covenant and relationship to protect their trustworthiness.

A covenant has a more sacred connotation than an agreement or a contract. It is the soul-bonding cement of commitment based on the ethics of the relationship, not the ironclad deal or lawyered pact. It is constructed of "do right," not just "protect mine." Being the standard-bearer for that code of commitment means serving from *who* you are, not just what you are supposed to do.

Look at your signage. Do your signs and messages sound like warm instructions to a valuable partner or like tough laws for a crafty criminal? Trust the customer, even when he or she is dead wrong. Trust is not about facts and figures; it is about feelings and perceptions. Get off the plain of who is right and who is wrong; being effective trumps being correct. Trust comes from a clear and present demonstration that you seek to know your customers' hopes and aspirations, not just their needs and expectations. A superficial interchange will always yield a shallow understanding. And the pursuit of understanding is the groundwater of trust.

Isadore Sharp, founder of Four Seasons Hotels, tells this story on the power of trust in his 2009 book, *Four Seasons: The Story of a Business Philosophy.*

Four Seasons Nevis [a tiny island in the Caribbean] was open a year . . . most of the people had never worked in a hotel before and many others had never worked anywhere. At the time, I was staying in one of our cottages along the beach and I ordered room service. A young lady came in with my order and set it up on the terrace.

"Where did you learn to do this," I asked her. "What job did you have before?" "Oh, I never worked before," she told me. "This was my first job, sir."

"Then how did you learn to do this? There are a lot of items, and everything's here, placed exactly as it should be." "Well, sir, they taught me everything."

"That's interesting," I said. "How did they do that?"

And she explained, "They let me take everything home for me to practice with my family."[2]

Four Seasons sees trust in much the same way as Stephen Covey—as "the glue of life." "It's the foundational principle that holds all relationships," Covey says. Every time a customer deals with a service provider, there is a trust walk involved. And it can begin, not by waiting for a long track record of experience, but by a leap of faith in customers that loudly proclaims, "Take my car!"

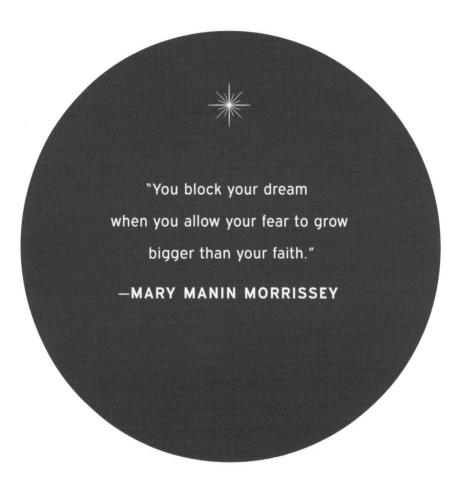

"You block your dream
when you allow your fear to grow
bigger than your faith."

—MARY MANIN MORRISSEY

Animators for Trust

Like a kaleidoscope that guarantees a spectacular experience every time you take a peek, innovative service is an experience that customers enjoy without looking over their shoulders or checking the math on their receipts.

- Trust is courageously opening up when conventional wisdom suggests defensively closing in. Boldly take a risk on relationships through openness, acceptance, and tenacity. Act like your customer is your best friend in need.

- Treat different customers differently. One-size-fits-all treatment shows ignorance of their uniqueness and indifference to learning about them. Find ways to make every customer's experience feel like it has his or her monogram on it.

- Make your customers feel they hit the service jackpot when they brought their issues or concerns to you. Sincerely thank them for bringing you their challenges. Then, go to work on it with the enthusiasm of a puppy with a new toy.

- No one ever got rich by stepping over dollars to pick up pennies. Focus on the relationship value rather than the transaction cost.

- Trusting service that touches customers' hearts comes from the overactive compassion in us and not from the hyperactive scrooge in us.

4

GENEROSITY

SERVE IT FORWARD

"Try to be the rainbow in someone's cloud."

—MAYA ANGELOU

Lawrence of Arabia won the academy award in 1962 for best picture. Given the current conflicts in the Middle East, I recently watched the four-hour movie to learn more about the cultural history of the area. Lieutenant T. E. Lawrence (played by Best Actor winner Peter O'Toole) was a British intelligence officer assigned to investigate the revolt of the Arabs against the Turks during World

War I. He embraced the culture and dress of the Arabs and organized a guerrilla army that for two years raided the Turks with surprise attacks.

In the early part of the movie, a poor Bedouin guide is hired to escort Lawrence across the desert to meet with Prince Faisal (played by Alec Guinness), the leader of the Arab revolt. (Faisal would ultimately become King of Greater Syria and King of Iraq, pushing for unity between the Sunni and Shiite Muslims). It was customary then for desert guides to be paid at the end of their assignment. Instead, at the beginning of their journey, Lawrence gave his military pistol to the guide—a gift of great value and pleasure for any Bedouin.

What followed was a powerful example of "serving it forward." The guide instantly gave Lawrence some of his food, provisions better suited to desert survival than the military rations Lawrence carried. The guide then assumed a mentoring role, revealing valuable desert survival secrets. The timing of Lawrence's unorthodox gift completely changed the dynamic of the relationship, with the Bedouin transforming from compliant servant into resourceful partner.

Customer service is a reciprocal act. Customers exchange money, time, and effort for goods and services. There are unwritten norms about how this mutual undertaking is performed. Customers are expected to communicate their needs; service providers are expected to indicate whether they can meet those needs. There are generally stated or implied expectations around speed, quality, cost, and so forth. Both parties assume a modicum of respect; both assume the exchange will employ a measure of fair play.

Adopt an Attitude of Abundance

Rosa's Fresh Pizza in Philadelphia started getting a lot of publicity after their decision to sell single slices of pizza for a dollar. But it didn't have to do with the price of the slice; it was about a customer-suggested idea for how to fund pizza for the homeless. It works like this: When customers buy pizza for themselves, they put a dollar in a container, write a message on a Post-it note, and stick it on the wall. Any homeless person can come into the store, take a Post-it note off the wall, and get a slice of pizza. Rosa's has given away thousands of slices.

The principle of abundance is about giving more than is expected. It is a proactive attitude of engulfing a relationship with emotional plenty without concern for reciprocity. Granted we cannot "give" our way to bottom-line success. An attitude of abundance is more the belief that if we employ a giver mentality, the customer will take care of the bottom line.

Abundance is a selfless gesture that changes the calculus of service from miserly subtraction to Midas-like addition. The sports world was uplifted in the 2016 Rio Olympics 5,000 meter heat when Abbey D'Agostino of the United States fell, causing her to trip up Nikki Hamblin of New Zealand, a fellow runner she did not know. D'Agostino could have regained her composure and continued toward the finish line. Instead, she worked to help Hamblin to her feet. But, D'Agostino's injured legs buckled in the attempt, and Hamblin returned the favor, helping D'Agostino. Neither runner resumed the race until both could successfully run. Because neither was at fault for the fall, both were allowed to race in the finals. "It is a moment," said Hamblin, "I will never, ever forget for the rest of my life." The cheering fans that watched the abundant gesture are not likely to forget it either.

The worth of a great customer experience requires a focus not on the transaction costs, but on the relationship value. Transaction costs are not irrelevant, but they can, if we are not careful, become destructively dominant. Loyal customers spend more money each year they are your customers. As advocates for your business, they become an extension of your sales and marketing efforts. Their word of mouth and "word of mouse" accolades influence prospects to become customers.

An abundance orientation has a magnetic impact on customers. It attracts them because it conveys to the customer the kind of unconditional positive regard that characterizes relationships at their best. Customers like the way they feel when dealing with service providers who have such an orientation. They feel valued, not used. They enjoy relationships with value and substance far more than encounters that are functional but hollow.

Deliver a Masterpiece

I took my beloved Lucchese western boots to McMillan's shoe repair store in Milledgeville, Georgia, for new soles and heels. Leaving them in the hands of a stranger was no doubt like leaving your hand-built, perfectly restored sports car with a new mechanic. When I returned a few days later, they were impeccably repaired and out of the boot emergency room.

"There was a crack in the leather on the left side of your left boot," said storeowner David Cooper. "It was just gonna get worse, so I took a piece of leather and repaired it."

I was thrilled with his obvious concern. "How much do I owe you for the extra repair?" I asked. His response was like the sound of great chorus. "You don't owe me nothing. I just wanted your beautiful boots to stay looking good and lasting a long time." I left him a very large tip.

Great service means caring so much about the experience you are authoring or the product you are caretaking that you are willing to invest more in it, purely in pursuit of the remarkable. Mr. Cooper went the extra mile, not because he sought my loyalty or my tip. He did it because he loved great boots! And anyone who loves the excellence of the service or product I am getting from them will always get my love right back.

Let your next customer encounter end with a personal investment in the best of what it could be. Shake hands as you thank your customer. Handwrite a thank you note to a key customer. Remember birthdays. Find a way to compliment your customer to their customer. Encourage reciprocal giving like the "Got a penny? Give a penny. Need a penny? Take a penny" signs you see near cash registers. Surprise your customer with an unexpected discount or a unique extra.

Generosity is the key to opening a door into a garden of opportunity for a more expansive relationship. Jacques Cousteau wrote, "It takes generosity to discover the whole through others. If you realize you are only a violin, you can open yourself up to the world by playing your role in the concert." Customers remember what you give to them long after they have forgotten what you take from them. Make what you gave them a memorable experience.

The backstory of *Lawrence of Arabia* was a man's search for meaning and self-understanding. T. E. Lawrence found in the Arabian Desert that, to quote Mahatma Gandhi, "The best way to find yourself is to lose yourself in the service of others." Give to your customers the best service you have, and their best will come back to you.

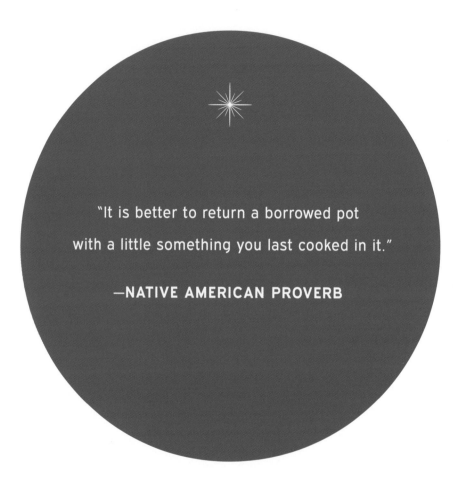

"It is better to return a borrowed pot
with a little something you last cooked in it."

—NATIVE AMERICAN PROVERB

Animators for Generosity

The word *kaleidoscope* comes from the amalgamation of three Greeks words— *kalos* (beauty), *eidos* (form), and *skopeo* (to examine or experience). Figuratively, it means, "experiencing constantly changing beautiful forms." Like a kaleidoscope that ensures the next array of color displayed will be even better than the last, let the service experience your customers have be one they view as bountifully beautiful.

- Don't wait for your customers to wear an "Ask Me about My Granddaughter" button; find ways to learn the target of their affinity, and add it to your list for attention.

- Know your customers well and aim for the response you believe they will value. It is the room service person delivering our breakfast who greeted our cat by name ("Good morning, Taco") when my wife and I stayed at the Four Seasons in Austin, Texas.

- Be your customer's mentor—escort them to insight and discovery rather than acting as an expert with secret information. Smart mentors guide; smart alecks gloat. Since learning is a door opened only from the inside, be the person your customers will want to invite in along with your wisdom.

- Change your call center farewells from a closed-ended "Is there anything else I can help you with?" to an open-ended and generous conclusion: "What else can I help you learn more about today?" Put QR (Quick Response) codes in lots of places—website, invoice, forms, products—with links to helpful learning information or videos.

- Generous service that truly helps sum up who you truly are is service laced with extras and given from a spirit that expects nothing in return.

TRUTH

NURTURE TOTAL CANDOR

"The pursuit of truth and beauty is a sphere of activity in
which we are permitted to remain children all our lives."

—ALBERT EINSTEIN

The Delta regional jet was full. As the plane backed away from the Jetway, the
flight attendant began her ritualistic safety spiel about seatbelts, sudden turbu-
lence, and the smoking rules. She ended by saying, "The flying time to Grand

Rapids will be two hours . . . no, it will be an hour and a half . . . no, actually, I don't know." The cabin erupted with laughter and applause.

What jolted the half-asleep plane full into boisterous cheering? Unscripted, raw honesty. We all loved her total candor and confident authenticity!

Customers love honesty, especially when circumstances might have others shading the truth or withholding the facts. JetBlue came back from chump to champ after the super long tarmac delay on a wintry day in Denver because the company CEO hid nothing. Toyota and Volkswagen got hammered because they did the opposite. And JetBlue, Toyota, and Volkswagen had sterling reputations before their visits to PR hell. Truth is a gauge on the face value of our dealings. It is the "cross your heart and hope to die" feature that leaves us not needing to look over our shoulders.

Use Candor That Cleanses

When I was in graduate school, one of the most provocative professors I had was Jerry Harvey. Jerry was a straight-talking Texan who used poignant, folksy stories to convey his powerful lessons. "The Abilene Paradox" was one of his stories that later became a book by the same title. His great book also contains the story of airline Captain Kohei Asoh, a veteran pilot of ten thousand flying hours with Japan Airlines.

In 1968, Captain Asoh mistakenly landed his DC-8 with ninety-six passengers and eleven crew members on board in the San Francisco Bay two and a half miles short of the runway. No one was harmed, and the aircraft was not damaged; in fact, most passengers were unaware they were in the water until they spotted rescue boats beside the plane.

The National Transportation Safety Board was obviously concerned and held a preliminary hearing to set the ground rules for what everyone thought would occupy months to ascertain who was at fault for this debacle. Reporters from all over the world came to cover the enquiry. Angry passengers, lawyers, pilot's associations, private citizens, representatives of foreign governments, and regulators all assembled en masse. Captain Asoh was the first witness at the hearing. Here is Harvey's description of what happened next.

"Asoh took the stand, and—as the story goes—the investigator in charge opened the hearing with the penetrating question: 'Captain Asoh, in your own words, can you tell us how you managed to land that DC-8 Stretch Jet two and a half miles out in the San Francisco Bay in perfect compass line with the runway?'

"Asoh's reply was: 'As you Americans say, Asoh f—k up!' With those words, the hearing was concluded. All had been said that could be said, and nothing more of consequence could be added."

Asoh was honest and told the truth. He didn't try to save face; he didn't even try to shroud the truth in a white lie.

White lies are defined as "a polite or harmless lie" and are distinguished from *black lies*—those with evil or malicious intent. But are they really polite or harmless? We use white lies when we compliment someone ("Your cake was delicious" or "That is an attractive dress") even though what we say is not what we truly believe. We tell a prospect we are pitching that the item she desires should arrive in two days even when we know four days is the most likely delivery time. We communicate to a vendor "the check is in the mail," and then quickly back up our white lie to make reality catch up with our falsehood.

White lies are unadulterated deception, regardless of their benevolent intent. They help us save face but do little to promote a solid relationship. We fool ourselves into believing white lies act as a governor on our otherwise hurtful bluntness. We use them in awkward moments when we lack the time or opportunity to craft an honest, but diplomatic, response. And we rely on them as a form of interpersonal cowardice.

Lies have a way of finding their way back to their target, forever tarnishing the relationship. "I'm not upset that you lied to me," wrote Friedrich Nietzsche, "I'm upset that from now on I can't believe you." And a larger challenge is that lies over time trap us in the conspiracy of our fabrications. "Oh, what a tangled web we weave, when first we practice to deceive!" wrote poet Walter Scott.

Invite Candor That Improves

"One of the surest signs of a bad or declining relationship with a customer is the absence of complaints. Nobody is ever *that* satisfied, especially not over an extended period of time. The customer is either not being candid or not being contacted." These words of Harvard professor and marketing guru Ted Levitt were tucked in his classic *Harvard Business Review* article "After the Sale is Over . . ."[3]

His message worried me for days! Here I was, striving to minimize customer irritation and ire only to have Levitt tell me that no complaints was something to be avoided, and it was my fault for not getting any! I was confused! Weren't we supposed to be seeking all As, zero defects, 100 percent, five stars, perfect CSIs, a hole-in-one? How can "getting more customer complaints" be a virtue? Can you imagine marching up to the boss or owner with the "good news" that complaints were up 23 percent, and therefore you needed a bigger budget, more staff, and a large salary increase?

Then, I got a wake-up call.

My wife and I enjoy a very open, honest partnership. Yet when the challenge of managing dual, fast-paced professional careers with typical family challenges worked counter to the late-at-night, no-kid-gloves honesty we desire, we had what we call a "you be frank and I'll be earnest" conversation. First, we privately listed "Likes" and "Needs Improvements." When she read my limitations out loud ("You sometimes focus so totally on your work that I don't get the attention

I need" or "You go into too much detail"), it had a rather sobering effect on us both! I began to appreciate why Levitt compared a quality customer relationship with a marriage. "The sale consummates the courtship at which point the marriage begins," wrote Levitt. "The absence of candor reflects the decline of trust and the deterioration of the relationship."

Value-unique customer relationships are coalitions laced in truth. Honesty and candor are seen as tools for growth rather than devices for disparagement. Partners serve each other straight talk mixed with compassion and care. The truth-seeking component of effective relationships is that which values candor and openness. It is the dimension that honors authenticity and realness.

Stop asking customers if they were "completely satisfied" with their experience. Were you "completely satisfied" with your honeymoon? Or would you evaluate it as awesome, extraordinary, or amazing? Seventy-five percent of customers who leave an organization to go with a competitor say they were "completely satisfied" with the one they abandoned. The customer's answer to "What is one thing we can do that would improve your experience?" can inform you on the truth about what customers need and expect.

This means you stop relying on surveys and start depending on great listening. Customer conversations instruct us on what we need to do today and tomorrow. No chef would serve day-old bread; no wise service providers would rely on rearview mirror survey data. Make all customer conversations an easy, neighborly dialogue. In the words of Winnie-the-Pooh, "It's more fun to talk with someone who doesn't use long, difficult words but rather short, easy words like 'What about lunch?'" And share what you learn so it fuels improvement that deepens customer loyalty.

Truth telling shortens the distance between people. It frees customers from anxiety and caution. It triggers a potent connection with the humanity in each of us. And in that space, we are quicker to forgive, more tolerant of error, and much more accepting of "Actually, I don't know." Honesty is not a "best policy." Honesty is a "best practice."

"If you tell the truth,

you don't have to remember anything."

—MARK TWAIN

Animators for Truth

As clear-cut and flawless as the symmetrical patterns created by the reflections of a kaleidoscope, innovative service is an honest expression of service attempting to be in its purest form.

- Tell customers what exact changes and improvements customer truth telling has inspired or informed. The more they perceive they have influence, the more likely they are to provide helpful candor.

- Everything in your customer's experience is personal. Corporate speak and sanitized legalese communication, by definition, violate that principle.

- When it comes to great listening, your customers are the only judges that count. If your customers don't believe you are a great listener, you aren't!

- Customers do not care about your policy, procedure, or authority. So don't bring it up. Instead, focus on finding a path to "Yes, we can!"

- Truthful service that truly saves people is laced with the unmistakable pursuit of honesty on both sides of the service equation.

MERCY

LET IT GO

"Teach me to feel another's woe, to hide the fault I see, that
mercy I to others show, that mercy show to me."

—ALEXANDER POPE

When I was twelve years old, I went to a weeklong summer camp. The camp had
a swimming area cordoned off from a lake with a diving board accessible via a
long wooden dock. The first morning, I went swimming with a couple of guys,

including Dwight Johnson. Dwight got suddenly excited and pushed me off the diving board.

Dwight was a mentally challenged boy and prone to getting unexpectedly aggressive. He likely assumed I would land in the lake. Instead, I hit the dock, severely spraining my right foot. It kept me physically grounded for the rest of camp. I was furious! And I stayed furious.

After we returned from camp, I plotted my revenge. I was going to catch Dwight alone and beat him up. For weeks, I contrived ways to lure him into my snare. One day, my dad said, "Dwight is still pushing you off that diving board; your anger is eating you up. What if you tried being Dwight's friend? He doesn't have many buddies because he's different."

The following Monday, I invited Dwight to sit with me in the lunchroom. He seemed surprised. Every day after that, I made the same request. I soon realized Dwight was a neat person. I also felt better about myself each time he joined me. On Friday, he gave me his dessert and said, "Thanks for being my friend. I'm sorry I pushed you off the diving board. It was an accident, but it was my fault."

Serve with Compassion

My tax records are organized in boxes and placed in a locked closet in our garage—one box per tax year. I recently needed to check a past tax return, so I retrieved the box for that year and brought it to my home office. When I opened it, I got a big surprise.

As soon as I lifted the cover, a gray field mouse leapt out of the box. It ran around my desk then quickly returned to the middle of the office floor a few feet in front of me and looked up at the box on my desk. I was stunned. This was not the behavior of a frightened mouse. I looked inside the box and learned the reason for her bravery: She had chewed a hole in the back of the cardboard box to turn my tax record repository into her birthing nest. There were baby mice inside—their eyes still unopened. Now, Ms. Mouse was risking her personal safety for their welfare.

I slowly took the box to the front door and placed it outside on the porch. I was turning around, wondering how I could enable her to rejoin her brood, when I discovered she had followed me to the front door. I left the door open so she could exit, and later that day, when I checked, the mice were gone. If those baby mice had been your customers, how much would you have sacrificed on their behalf?

Several weeks later, I was in a retail store and overheard a clerk complaining about a grouchy customer: "He is always so short and cranky!" As I was checking out, I heard her team member say, "You are right. But what you don't know is Mr. Simpson lost his wife last month and his family lives several states away. We need to take care of him even if he doesn't act like he wants our help." That's what Ms. Mouse would have said too.

Every service provider on the planet at some point gets to encounter an angry customer. Interpersonal hiccups can ruin anyone's day. But I will let you in on a little secret that will make all the difference. Mercy allows us to let go. It is the medicine for healing broken relationships with upset customers. Responding quickly is important. And letting customers hear empathy and understanding can communicate a kinship that signals to customers that they are dealing with an ally and not an adversary.

Anger is not a primary behavior; it is a secondary behavior. The primary behavior is fear. What we see on the outside might be fury, but in the mind of the angry person is a fear of being a victim. What does *victim* really mean? It could mean many things:"I will look stupid," "I will lose control," "You will win and I will lose," "I will lose now but I'll lose even more next time." You get the idea. Meeting anger with acceptance, humility, and empathy invites your assailant out of their anger to greater understanding, resolution, and a wholesome relationship.

Innovative service is not about serving the easy, polite customers; it is about taking great care of customers who, for many reasons, do not have their eyes open at the time. Start by listening to learn. That means complete absorption, curiosity, and caring without an agenda. Do not listen to plan your counter attack. Be willing to be wrong in your assumption. Be open to being off guard. Communicate total humility and acceptance. "I am so sorry that happened," signals to customers they are valued rather than communicating they are wrong. Emotional surrender does not imply weakness or white flags; it courageously communicates a concern for a win-win solution that strengthens instead of separates.

Be the Rising Tide

My business partner, John Patterson, and I were teaching a customer service class to a group of union employees—teamsters, carpenters, and electricians—at an organization in midtown New York City. The audience had a reputation for being very tough on instructors and livid about being forced to attend. One hostile participant arrived and curtly announced our class was a complete waste and he would sit "wherever the hell he wanted."

We elected to meet hostility with respect, anger with acceptance, and posturing with affirmation. Each time a participant indignantly issued a defiant statement, it was met with warmth and compassion. There was no parental behavior exhibited, even with sophomoric attempts to show off to peers. Halfway through the class, the entire group was engaged and enjoying the experience.

But, here's the best part. Several of the attendees came up at the end of class to apologize for their behavior and that of their peers. With tears in their eyes, some talked about it being the best class they had ever attended. Then the most militant participant made a show-stopping statement: "You guys looked past our faults and saw our gifts." The class was great, not because of our prowess as instructors, but because they were forgiven. Just as a rising tide raises all boats, a character-based forgiving response elevates the quality of all relationships.

One of the most powerful scenes in Shakespeare's play *The Merchant of Venice* occurs when moneylender Shylock takes to court Antonio for defaulting on his loan. He demands a pound of flesh, as stipulated in their loan agreement as the penalty. The heroine of the play, Portia, disguises herself as a judge, hears the case, and renders a powerful rebuttal (and a clever judgment).

> The quality of mercy is not strain'd,
> It droppeth as the gentle rain from heaven
> Upon the place beneath: it is twice blest;
> It blesseth him that gives and him that takes:
> 'Tis mightiest in the mightiest: it becomes
> The throned monarch better than his crown;
> His scepter shows the force of temporal power,
> The attribute to awe and majesty,
> Wherein doth sit the dread and fear of kings;
> But mercy is above this sceptered sway;

It is enthroned in the hearts of kings,

It is an attribute to God himself.

Portia's famous speech rings as true today as it did when it was written in the sixteenth century. Poet Hannah More declared forgiveness the economy of the heart. "Forgiveness," she wrote, "saves the expense of anger, the cost of hatred, and the waste of spirits."

Mercy is to interpersonal discord what chicken soup is to a bad cold when you were young . . . but with a twist. It was not chicken soup that helped you feel on your path to wellness. It was *your mother's* chicken soup, made with caring, fidelity, and full expectation of your improvement. Mercy's presence in a relationship comes when it is being tested, challenged, or disputed. Mercy is more than forgiveness. It is a relationship surrendering to what it could be rather than controlling or containing what it is. It is neither an expression of pity nor an air of tolerance. Rather, it is expanding the boundaries of the relationship to allow it to reform, renew, and reward.

"I think tolerance and acceptance and love is something that feeds every community."[4]

—LADY GAGA

Animators for Mercy

It can be somewhat challenging to get binoculars into focus. Each lens needs its own adjustments to get the lenses to accurately focus together. My young granddaughters always ask me to focus the binoculars for them. But the kaleidoscope seems suited for users without regard to expertise or experience. It is an egalitarian joy toy—my eight-year-old granddaughter is instantly an expert without worrying about making a mistake or needing help. Mercy is about encouraging and empowering a relationship so it can become focused.

- When things go wrong for customers, they only value your competence after they have witnessed your compassion. Great service recovery lets a disappointed or angry customer know you are there to fix, not to fight.

- Let your customers vent their frustration or anger by being a patient, empathetic listener. Before you can fill your customers' emotional tank with positive energy, you must permit them to drain off their negative energy.

- When your customers experience a hiccup, they are crystal clear on how you should respond. The only way you can match or exceed their expectations is to know them.

- Assume the most important people in your life—your parents, significant other, or children—could watch you in action dealing with challenging customers. What valuable lessons would they learn from your actions?

- *Taking the high ground* is a military expression for assuming a position achieved only through sacrifice and valor. Service that is profound is service founded in mercy; in taking the interpersonal high ground that lets go of bias, prejudice, and judgment. It means acceptance and patience. Let your most challenging customer be your training ground for practicing mercy.

ALLIANCE

STAY...ON PURPOSE

"Partnership is a verb disguised as a noun.
It is a force released, 'un-nouned,'
when dreams connect and service is gracefully given."

—FROM *CUSTOMERS AS PARTNERS*

It was a gorgeous early morning in midtown Memphis, Tennessee. I was hungry for an old-fashioned breakfast and tired of the hotel restaurant menu. Plus, the evening before, the sole of my right dress shoe elected to separate from the shoe without so much as a friendly warning. So, I was also hungry for a shoe expert to get me ready for a late-morning engagement.

Walking down Main Street a couple of blocks from the hotel, right shoe in hand, I encountered Mr. Chester in front of the Down to Earth Barber Shop. He had a broad smile, a shiny bald head, impish eyes, and a face likely contoured by many long, hard miles.

"I am looking for a great place for breakfast," I told him.

"That would be the Blue Plate Café just around the corner," he answered without hesitation. Staring at my dress shoe, he continued, "What's with the shoe?" I was so impressed with his warm, confidant style I had almost forgotten my cargo.

"And I am also looking for someone who can repair this shoe in a hurry," I told him. The shop behind him was dark and noticeably closed.

He proudly announced, "I'm the shoe man! I'm Mr. Chester."

I was feeling lucky. "What time do you open?" I queried.

His answer was laced with bright charisma. "Tell you what. If you'll buy me a cup of coffee at the Blue Plate, I'll have your shoe repaired by the time you finish your breakfast." It seemed like a fair deal.

We walked a half block to the restaurant; he got his coffee to go and disappeared. A half hour later, I was walking into his shoe repair corner of the Down to Earth Barber Shop. His face now looked like that of an artist who had just completed a masterpiece. The right shoe was perfect—complete with a fresh shine! As I left the shop, he called out, "Please come back to see me again, partner!"

Partner seemed like the perfect moniker for the brief relationship we enjoyed. He could have said, "Shop opens at 9:00." He might have said, "I can have it ready by next Tuesday." And the transaction could have occurred with a normal trade—a shoe repair in exchange for twenty dollars. But he charmed me into buying him a cup of coffee and then rewarded my generosity with what he could offer—a shoeshine at no extra cost. It was an alluring and irresistible alliance.

Practice Floating Reciprocity

Most customer relationships are exercises in confidant deference. They reflect "the customer is always right" or "the customer is king" mentality. This does not mean service providers are servant-like; customers enjoy servers with confidence. But it does imply the service provider accedes to the customer's wishes and needs while demonstrating a self-assured attitude. Mr. Chester was very confident; he was also noticeably respectful. He turned acquiescence into mutuality.

What changed the encounter from a routine transaction to a valued partnership was his encouragement of interdependence—he would open up early in exchange for a cup of diner coffee. I never got the impression he could not afford what he requested. Instead, he seemed to be inviting me to put some skin in the game.

Great partnerships care about fairness, not a perfect fifty-fifty split. Who knows if the cost of a cup of coffee matched the charge for a shoeshine? I was unconcerned about tit for tat, and so was Mr. Chester. Great partnerships are about floating reciprocity and are grounded in an optimism that says, "It will all balance out in the end," even if the concept of "end" is rather imprecise. Their energy is on abundance, not on scarcity; giving takes precedence over scorekeeping.

Great partnerships have built-in shock absorbers. They affirm their relationships more through ebb and flow than give and take. They encourage elbow room rather than close inspection. They seek ways to open rather than means to close. They expand and unfold in their acceptance; little bumps in the rocky road of relationship are absorbed without attention. Instead of nitpicking details, they work to roll with normal imperfections; more like a willow than a pole. When customers put too much energy into little details, surprise them by joyfully yielding to their too-loud demands.

Examine your business practices. Do you make customers go to the nth degree to get what they need? Are there barriers that make it difficult to get an unusual request fulfilled? Try calling someone in your unit. Disguise your voice and ask for something unique or out of the ordinary. Do your associates expand or recoil? Do they tell or do they ask? Take a "The answer is yes, what is your question?" approach to signal that assertive acceptance is more virtuous than stoic tolerance. It lets employees show the customer optimistic fluidness, not self-sacrificing indulgence.

Be the Contract

Business cards are like a corporate signature. Some have the flamboyance of John Hancock. Some are cute, like they were designed by someone's interior decorator. Some have cool logos on the front or clever statements on the back. A few have unique shapes. Most are colorful. All are the reflection of someone's idea of what the organization wanted to project to the marketplace. Giving someone your business card is an invitation for a future connection.

The service you provide is a kind of business card. It telegraphs what you want your customers to remember. Your service reflects the tone, color, and charm you want customers to recollect when they think of you and your organization. It is your signature statement that says, "This is who I am; will you come back again?" How can your service be a unique and memorable invitation?

Partners don't put much energy into contracts. They value clear agreements and mutual understanding. I had complete faith I would not have to wait on my shoe repair after breakfast. Great partners' strong, fair-play ethics fuel their drive to always do the right thing. Think about it: Where did contracts originate? They emerged from a betrayal of the fairness doctrine—someone cut the candy bar and also took the first piece!

We live in an era of razor-thin margins, bottom-line obsession, and aggressive cost control. Solid metrics sometimes trump good manners. When the "balance the books" bean counters search for all the pennies in customer transactions, they risk losing the dollars of loyal customers who desire a relationship with a bit more give in it. But what customers long to experience most is the sentiment borne in "Please come back to see me again, partner."

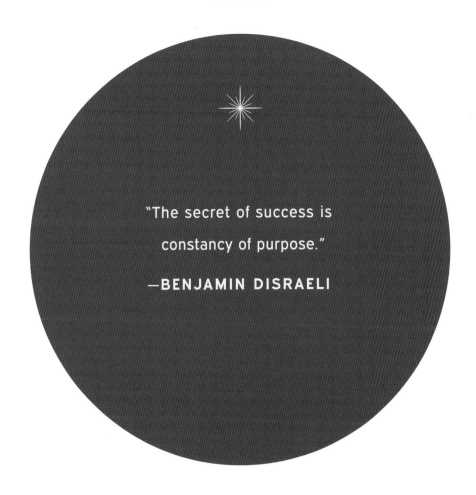

"The secret of success is constancy of purpose."

—BENJAMIN DISRAELI

Animators for Alliance

A remarkable feature of a kaleidoscope is the way it invites you to share the beauty you see inside. We sometimes think of a kaleidoscope as a solitary toy. Yet, if there are others standing nearby, you find yourself holding the kaleidoscope very steady so you won't change the pattern as you pass it around saying, "Wow, looky here!" Value-unique service is so moving you want it to be shared, not just delivered. You want it to enfold, not just assist.

- When you ask your customers for help, only ask for what is reasonable—a request appropriate to make of a loyal customer. Provide customers with a brief background when making a request for assistance.

- Help your customers feel they are in charge of their experience and you are the ringmaster of their enchantment. "What works for you?" signals an invite to insight.

- Help your customers become the world's smartest buyers by hardwiring learning into every customer encounter.

- Assertive helping is as important to service as assertive hustling is in an athletic competition. Customers feel valued when they witness your initiative and swiftness.

- Service that deeply moves customers is service that ensures customers view participation as a collective, egalitarian effort. Customers enjoy being a partner; they do not relish being your servant.

EASE

TAKE CARE OF FLOW

"In order to succeed in business and differentiate yourself
from competitors, you do not have to be 1000% better
at one thing; you have to be 1% better at 1000 things!"
—JAN CARLZON, FORMER CEO OF SAS AIRLINES

Max Gentry is a happy camper! Literally! Max is a dog that belongs to my friend Todd Gentry and his family. When a trip is on their calendar, Max goes to camp at the Paws Awhile Pet Resort at the Animal Medical Center of Cumming, Georgia.

Max gets to play with his friends in one of four play parks—Max likes the Pawnee Mountain Park because it has a tall fort. He can bark and catch a Frisbee from up top!

But this is not about Max. Max may be the customer, but the Gentry's pay the bill! The Gentry family misses Max when they are away. And they worry about how Max is doing. Is he lonely? Is he eating properly? Does he miss them? But, their worries are short-lived because Paws Awhile sends them peace of mind through their fun and innovative daily communications.

Every day, the Gentry family gets a text with messages like, "Max's enjoyed playing with his new friend, Lucky, today" or "Max had a blast running wild and getting lots of hugs during his petting session" or "Max and Zoey took a long nap in the sun in the yard." The best part is the happy photos that accompany the daily texts. Each pet is assigned a concierge and referred to as a VIP, not a pet.

But the great service experience does not stop there. When the Gentry family picks up Max, he is always wearing an attractive bandana. There is a detailed report card outlining his entire stay, along with photos of Max with his friends to take home and post on his bulletin board! Max gets unforgettable service, and so does the Gentry family.

Ease is more than an effortless experience. It means an experience without angst and worry. It is the execution of smooth, drag-free service, much like the flow of a river after a rain. It requires well-being management and careful attention to the details. Customers don't care how much you know until they know how much you care. Value-unique caring can turn an emerging oops into an opportunity for magic.

God Is in the Details

Innovative service is not just about responding to what customers say; it is an exercise in empathy—sensing through the emotional lens of a customer. It is making the customer's path to an outcome comfortable and compassionate. It takes up-to-the-minute customer intelligence on complaints and concerns coupled with in-the-moment insight into the anthropology of the customer's encounter. Time, space, sensory cues, and language are all rich trails to helpful discovery.

Why do we put bent cans of vegetables back on the grocery store shelf? Why do inexperienced flyers take out flight insurance before boarding the plane but don't bother with taxi insurance when boarding a cab? Why do we FedEx or UPS a large check when speed of arrival is not a requirement? An important part of understanding service is that it involves perceptual features that, if missed, mangled, or jeopardized, trigger alarm, not anger. Experiences characterized as frightful are remembered long after irritating moments are forgotten.

"God is in the details," wrote renowned architect Ludwig Mies van der Rohe. Customers use detail management as an indicator of the individual or organization's commitment to delivering a positive service experience. But there is a more profound element of detail management that often stays hidden. While server and customer might both agree certain outcomes occurred, assessment of the experience that accompanied that outcome is totally in the eye of the beholder. A customer's perceptions about a bus driver with obvious alcohol breath, for example, are not just about the driver's personal habits. As customers, our perceptions can take us way past what we observe to what we conclude.

When John Longstreet—now executive director of the Pennsylvania Hotel and Restaurant Association—was the general manager of the Harvey Hotel in

Plano, Texas, he realized the taxi drivers who transported his guests to the airport after their stay were an informational gold mine. John reasoned that Harvey guests would more likely volunteer their impressions and be candid with their taxi driver than to answer the smiling desk clerk's question, "How was your stay?" So he set up periodic focus group meetings with the drivers.

Their conversations revealed subtle aspects of the guests' experiences rarely found on a comment card. The smell of slightly scorched towels from overheated dryers triggered concerns about a potential hotel fire, a poorly lighted parking lot potentially brought worries about safety in hotel hallways, and dust balls under the bed could conjure up images of unwelcome bugs in the room. These "minors" were actually warning signals that spotlighted potential "majors" in jeopardy.

Make It Easy

Customer journeys is the new label for the Cycle of Service and Moments of Truth concepts the late Ron Zemke crafted in his bestselling books *Service America* and *The Service Edge*. But there is more than "walking in the customer's shoes" needed to diagram the trail of experiences innovative service providers go through to meet a need or request. Try as we may, we know way too much about our internal processes and assume too much about our customers to effectively wear their shoes. What this means is that we need customers to help accurately describe each step in their journey, how they feel about that step, and ways to make it easy for them to participate in that service expedition. It's like the Polish proverb says: "A guest sees more in an hour than the host in a year."

Invite your customer on a detail treasure hunt. You can set it up like this: "Thank you for being our customer. We are trying to see more details that we don't see (because we work here and take them for granted) that you do see. We call this our *detail treasure hunt*. While you are here, try to spot details that might be a bit of a turnoff or negative that you think we might not see. If you spot a detail we were not aware of . . . one no other customer has mentioned . . . we will give you a free dessert (or whatever prize you see fit)."

Walk with customers like a reporter covering a race or a mountain climb. Ask questions that reveal emotions, not just facts. Seek insight directly from customers into ways to make that path facile, comfortable, and free of uncertainty. Go back again with your notes from your customers and isolate each sense for another inspection. Pay attention only to what a customer might smell, touch, hear, or feel. Sometimes the cacophony of sensory input can drown out a dissonant component of the customer's experience we otherwise notice. Conduct customer forensics by interviewing lost customers to uncover the real reasons they departed, not what they reported as they exited. If they are convinced that you are there to learn and your dialog is not a disguised attempt to win them back, they will reveal their hidden secrets.

The key to innovative service is appreciating its complexity, understanding its impact, and paying attention to the details that trigger customer angst and discomfort. Smart organizations focus on the majors when it comes to ensuring customers reliably get exactly what they expect from the organization. The best service organizations also focus on the minors—taking the initiative to care for and protect the subtle but vital fine points of value-unique service.

"It isn't the mountain ahead

that wears you out,

it is the grain of sand in your shoe."

—ROBERT W. SERVICE, Canadian poet

Animators for Ease

Kaleidoscopes are like "happy processes"—a phrase a client coined to describe service methods and procedures that are easy to use, easy to maintain, and work well with each other. With a simple turn of the animator and a peep through the eyepiece, you get a glorious pageantry of magnetism.

- Ease is about comfort, not just stress-free service. Be your customers' pathfinder to ease by examining their experience through their eyes, not yours.

- Become famous for ease of access. If the Publishers Clearing House Prize Patrol were calling you about your check, you would not want them to end up in your voice mail.

- Disney World does not do "partial magic." Make every tiny part of your customer's experience consistent with how you want to be remembered.

- Encourage complaints. Keep a log on concerns in order to spot trends, provide early warnings, or conduct root cause analysis to learn what creates customer disappointment and anxiety.

- Service with ease that makes customers feel they deeply matter relies on a well-calibrated, always-turned-on customer anxiety meter to activate removal of even the tiniest angst from each customer's experience.

9

PASSION

BE ALL THERE

"Without courage, all other virtues lose their meaning."
—WINSTON CHURCHILL

Like a bolt of lightning, Jamaican Usain Bolt streaked into the history books as the fastest person on the planet. He is the first person to hold the world record in both the 100-meter and 200-meter dash. He won three gold medals at the 2016 Rio Olympics and made it look like a jubilant jog in the park. We marveled at his athletic talent as he turned on the afterburners every time a competitor gained on him. He always smiled before he ran, while he ran, and after he crossed the finish line. He runs with unbridled passion.

But the most amazing part of Bolt's achievement was his special connection with the spectators. They loved him, and he loved them right back. When he gave his signature pose like an archer pointing an arrow at the sky, they screamed. And when he held his finger to his lips for silence at the start of a race, they delightfully complied.

Service with passion is the effect of an energized connection that inspires, enchants, and influences. It is the intersection where the best in a service provider meets the best in a customer. A deliberate and cherished gift, it does more than yield loyalty on both sides; it harvests deep respect, admiration, and devotion. Fundamentally, it is serving at its purest; relationship building at its deepest.

Most customer relationships do not end with a storm of sound and fury. Most do not end in a fit of dissonance or from caustic conflict. Most "vanilla" to death. It is death by indifference, monotony, and negligence. Dissect the word *passion* and you actually get three words—*pass-I-on*. It is passing on the best of who you to someone else. Rollo May said, "There is an energy field between people. When we reach out in passion it is met with an answering passion and changes the relationship forever."[5] But what special alchemy transforms a functional interaction between a service provider and a customer into something that is pure gold?

Passion Is Unbridled

One of the most memorable lines from the movie *Steel Magnolias* came from the character Shelby Latcherie (played by Julia Roberts), a courageous and passionate diabetic expectant mother facing the life-threatening potential of giving birth. "I would rather have thirty minutes of wonderful," she says, "than a lifetime of nothing special." Passion-filled service providers find the thrill of a "victorious" outcome so compelling they are willing to risk the potential of customer rejection, indifference, and failure. They trust their confident glow to light up the relationship and chaperone it to greatness.

So how do you serve with obvious passion? Be boldly optimistic about the service outcome. Go into each encounter with the expectation it will be exceptional. Target each customer encounter as a stage on which to parade the person you are at your best. Tell your doubts, reservations, cautions, and reserve to be a spectator in the cheap seats and not your noisy coach on the sideline. Imagine a spectacular conclusion and pursue that vision with every fiber of your being. Recall the strength you exerted to claim a vital victory in your past, and summon that same boundless power to propel you to this remarkable outcome.

Passion Is Invitational

"Manners," said Usain Bolt, "is the key thing. Say, for instance, when you're growing up, you're walking down the street; you've got to tell everybody 'good morning.' Everybody. You can't pass one person."[6] Customers can perceive extreme confidence and courageous assertiveness as arrogance or selfishness. The antidote to misinterpreted superiority is inclusion. We vicariously ran with Bolt because he invited us to be a part of his triumph. We shared his joy as if it was our own. He compelled us to smile back. Bolt told a reporter, "When people see your personality come out, they feel so good, like they actually know who you are."[7]

Make service feel to your customers like a treasure hunt for an incredible prize. Ask questions that yield deep insight not just superficial information. Replace informing with inquiry. Make problem-solving a joint action of discovery, not a solo act of an expert with all the answers. Mutuality can turn deference into a partnership, caution into collaboration.

Passion Is Empathetic

Empathy is grounded in the biblical injunction to "Love thy neighbor as thyself." It literally means "in-feeling" or the ability to understand another's feelings. Relationship strength is not spawned by "misery loves company" sympathy; it comes through "I've been there too" identification. Empathy is a confident expression of kinship and an engraved invitation to partner.

Seek to find the echo of you in your customer. Intrigue your customers through your sincere curiosity and eagerness to learn the motive behind their need and the logic beneath their request. Don't just stand in their shoes; help your customer feel you in their shoes. Listen with a quiet mind, as if what your customer is communicating will be the last statement, requiring no retort, clarification, or correction.

Passion-filled service is fundamentally about commitment. It is the outcome that results from the fervor to be all-in, to serve without reluctance. W. H. Murray, in his book, *The Scottish Himalayan Expedition*, wrote: "Until one is committed, there is hesitancy, the chance to draw back, always ineffectiveness. The moment one definitely commits oneself, then Providence moves, too. All sorts of things occur to help one that would never otherwise have occurred." Goethe called that unbridled commitment "boldness" and wrote: "Whatever you can do, or dream you can, begin it. Boldness has genius, power, and magic in it." Just ask Usain Bolt!

Every person, unit, and organization on the planet has a spirit laser. It is the amount of joy-filled light, energy, and attentiveness one concentrates on another. And people or organizations whose spirit lasers register a high candlepower have a huge emotional connection with the recipients of that light. *Candlepower* is largely an obsolete term but is still sometimes used to describe the luminous intensity of high-powered flashlights and spotlights. So, if the candlepower of the customer experiences you help create were unbundled like the colors of the rainbow, what might they contain? Would they contain eye hugs—powerful looks of attentiveness and affirmation? Would they imprint your John Hancock on your customer's memory?

We started this book with "Enchantment" and ended with "Passion." Like the inner substance of the animated, emotional delight of peering through a kaleidoscope, these "colored stones" are bookends to creating experiences that truly change people. But the root of the word *innovating* in the book subtitle is the Latin word *nova,* which means "new." *New* means change, and change can upset the comfort and predictability of the status quo. People around you have invested and are invested in the status quo. Innovative service can require bravery and a pioneering spirit.

Singer Katy Perry said, "I feel like my secret magic trick that separates me from a lot of my peers is the bravery to be vulnerable and truthful and honest."[8] It's that bravery that can lead to greatness. "Greatness," wrote James Harvey Robinson, "in the last analysis, is largely bravery—courage in escaping from old ideas and old standards

and respectable ways of doing things." Today's customers long for service greatness expressed in ways that enrich their lives as it fulfills their needs.

The most famous kaleidoscope in history was not designed by kaleidoscope inventor Dr. David Brewster of Edinburgh, Scotland, but by Charles Bush of Boston, Massachusetts. Bush's kaleidoscope used thirty-five objects of various colors and shapes, some of which were filled with liquid-containing air bubbles. And the air bubbles in these liquid-filled objects (called *ampules*) would move through the liquid, even when the kaleidoscope was held motionless. Innovative service is like that, an experience in animated surprise, a small but significant addition to great service that turns quality into wonder and merit into magic. Bottom line: It creates a customer who is profoundly moved, not just properly served.

"One person with passion

is better than forty people merely interested."

—E. M. FORSTER

Animators for Passion

You will never see an ugly kaleidoscope. Their decorative exterior is a reminder of what your mother told you: "You never get a second chance to make a good first impression." Let your passion project to customers a charming and inviting demonstration.

- Movies have trailers; symphonies have overtures. Look for ways to create a sense of happy anticipation—an exciting buildup before service delivery.

- Identify a service "souvenir"—a small, delightful takeaway that could extend the customer's experience beyond adieu.

- Become extraordinary on those things that matter most to your customers. Own the customer's moment with you.

- Listen to learn, not to make a point. Customers will indirectly tell you ways to personalize their experience. Thank your customers like you really mean it.

- Passionate service that truly saves people is delivered with energy, focused attention, and a zeal to elevate the candlepower on customers' experiences.

THE SOUVENIR
—TOP THAT!

Jerry Lee Lewis (aka The Killer) has been a wild country music singer performing for over sixty years! His performances continue to electrify with acrobatic

boogie-woogie piano playing and wall-to-
wall nonstop passion. Having attended his
concerts more than once, I have watched
him amaze huge audiences with his talent,
versatility, and willingness to be experimen-
tal. He is eighty-plus and still performing!

In the 1989 movie *Great Balls of Fire*, Jerry
Lee, played by Dennis Quaid, is told by the
show's producer that he will have to perform
on stage *before* the great Chuck Berry. Lewis

balks and insists that he close the show, not Berry. Jerry Lee's agent loses the argu-
ment since it is in Berry's contract that he close all shows in which he performs.

Jerry Lee relents and delivers a crowd-pleasing, dance-in-the-aisles show. Near the end of his wild rendition of "Great Balls of Fire," he sets the grand piano on fire and continues to play. Walking off the stage with a cocky air as the audience screams for more and the police struggle to keep adoring fans off the stage, he turns to Chuck Berry and calmly says, "Follow that, Killer!" Complete bafflement is the look on Berry's face.

Customers today sometimes receive "pianos-on-fire" experiences. Over 150 million people have been awed by a Cirque du Soleil performance. Over 40 million people went to Disney's Magic Kingdom, Epcot, and Animal Kingdom last year alone! And subconsciously, these customers are looking at your customer experience and thinking, *Follow that, Killer!*

Winning organizations deliver service experiences that get people talking, not just walking! Every organization cares about customer retention. But growth comes from customer advocates—devoted fans that not only return with their funds but also come back with their friends. People do not brag about good service; they boast about unique, captivating service experiences. And with all the competitors out there thinking up new ways to "set their pianos on fire," the time has come to top your good customer experiences with innovative service delivered with sparkles!

THANKS, GRACIAS, GRAZIE, MERCI, VIELEN DANK, XIÈXIÈ, AND ARIGATOU

Someone once asked me, "How do you write a book?" The bad boy in me, remembering the many late nights and weekends, wanted to answer: "One word at a time!" While true, such a terse answer fails to capture the magic and mystery of the writing process. Books are not written like a high school term paper. They are inspired—sometimes in a mystical fashion that causes the author to feel much more like a scribe taking dictation from a spirit much wiser than the pounder of the computer keyboard. The words arrive as a special gift an author feels privileged to have been chosen to record.

The inspiration for conceiving and birthing a book comes from special sources. This is the place I wish to say thanks, gracias, grazie, merci, etc., to those who inspired this book. My granddaughters—Kaylee, Annabeth, and Cassie—remind me of the enchanting power of innocence, purity, and wonderment. They inspire me to use such valuable search tools when seeking insight and ingenuity.

My clients challenge me with their thoughtful questions and stimulating interactions, enticing me to dig deeper into the mysteries of innovative service. A special graduate school professor, Leonard Nadler, encouraged me long ago to turn my graduate papers for his classes into articles suitable for publishing. I published several while in graduate school and caught the writing bug. As a special gift, he agreed to coauthor my first book, generously sharing his renown with a newbie and professional unknown.

Leslie Stephen is the extraordinary vernacular engineer who converted my partially baked ideas and randomly constructed concepts into the organized, fluid epistle you hold in your hands. This is our eighth book together. Candid feedback and creative ideas also came from my business partner (and coauthor of several previous books), John Patterson, as well as Dave Basarab and Dave Brookmire. Ray Bard helped with the title and subtitle.

The great folks at Greenleaf Book Group in Austin, Texas, turned a colorless stack of manuscript paper filled with errors and typos into a magnificent work of which I am exceedingly proud. They are truly an author's publisher. Of special note are my editor, Lindsey Clark, my cover designer, Kimberly Lance, my production manager, Tyler LeBleu, and my acquisition liaison, Justin Branch. This is my second book with Greenleaf—a testament to their artistry and profession-alism. A hat tip as well to my great publicity firm, Weaving Influence (especially Rachel Royer), for their suggestions on titling and cover design.

But, the Best Inspiration Award goes to my wife of over fifty years, Dr. Nancy Rainey Bell. Her unconditional love daily reminds me that falling in love with your life purpose is as important as staying in love with your life partner. She has been a right-between-the-eyes critic when my healthy ego got a bit (maybe more than a bit) out of bounds. She has been patient and encouraging when my preoccupation with my work took control over a healthier balance in life.

To all of you, arigatou, xièxiè, vielen dank, merci, thanks, etc.

Note: Portions of this book have previously appeared in my guest blogs for SwitchandShift.com and my website, chipbell.com. The story about Howard Perdue in chapter 2 was adapted from my book, *Customers as Partners*.[9] The screenplay quoted from *Walk the Line* was used with written permission from Twentieth Century Fox. The quote from *The Abilene Paradox* was used with writ-ten permission from John Wiley and Sons. All photos were used with permission.

A WORD ABOUT QR CODES

If you are unfamiliar with them, a QR code (or quick response code) is a two-dimensional barcode that can be read using smartphone applications or dedicated QR reading devices. A QR code links directly to videos, emails, websites, phone numbers, text, and more. Go to the App Store and download a QR reader.

NOTES

1. Seth Godin, "The Irrational Thing about Trust," *Seth's Blog* (blog), February 28, 2016, http://sethgodin.typepad.com/seths_blog/2016/02/the–surprising–thing–about–trust.html.

2. Isadore Sharp, *Four Seasons: The Story of a Business Philosophy* (New York: Penguin Group, 2009), 185.

3. Theodore Levitt, "After the Sale Is Over . . ." *Harvard Business Review,* September 1983, 88–94.

4. Noah Michelson, "Lady Gaga Discusses Activism, Outing and Reading Her Male Alter Ego, Jo Calderone, as a Transgender Man," *The Huffington Post*, February 2, 2016.

5. Rollo May, *Love and Will* (New York: Dell Publishing, 1969), 312.

6. Belmont and Belcourt Biographies, *Usain Bolt: An Unauthorized Biography*, (New York: Price World Publishing, 2012).

7. Ibid.

8. Nardine Saad, "Katy Perry Is 'Positive' after Brand Divorce, 'Prism,' John Mayer," *LA Times*, December 9, 2013.

9. Chip Bell, *Customers as Partners* (San Francisco: Berrett-Koehler Publishing, 1994), 61–62.

ABOUT THE AUTHOR

Chip R. Bell is a senior partner with the Chip Bell Group, LLC and manages their office near Atlanta. A renowned keynote speaker, he has served as consultant, trainer, or speaker to such major organizations as GE, IBM, Microsoft, USAA, Marriott, Lockheed Martin, Cadillac, KeyBank, Ritz-Carlton Hotels, United Technologies, Caterpillar, Eli Lilly, JCPenney, Verizon Wireless, Nationwide, Hertz, Accenture, Home Depot, WestRock, Cornell University, Harley-Davidson, and Victoria's Secret. Prior to starting a consulting firm in the early 1980s, he was Director of Management and Organization Development for NCNB (now Bank of America). Additionally, Dr. Bell was a highly decorated infantry unit commander in Vietnam with the elite 82nd Airborne and a guerilla tactics instructor at the United States Army Infantry School.

Chip is the author or coauthor of twenty-one books, many of which are national and international best sellers. Some of his previous books include

Sprinkles: Creating Awesome Experiences Through Innovative Service (winner of a 2014 GoldenInk Award), *The 9½ Principles of Innovative Service*, *Wired and Dangerous* (coauthored with John Patterson and a winner of a 2012 Axiom Award as well as a 2011 Independent Publishers IPPY Award), *Take Their Breath Away* (also with John Patterson), *Managers as Mentors* (with Marshall Goldsmith and winner of the Athena Award), *Magnetic Service* (with Bilijack Bell and winner of the 2004 Benjamin Franklin Book Award), *Managing Knock Your Socks Off Service* (with Ron Zemke), *Service Magic* (also with Ron Zemke), *Dance Lessons: Six Steps to Great Partnerships* (with Heather Shea), and *Customers as Partners.* He has appeared live on *CNBC, CNN, Fox Business Network, Bloomberg TV, ABC,* and *NPR,* and his work has been featured in *Fortune, Bloomberg Businessweek, Forbes, Wall Street Journal, USA Today, Huffington Post, Inc. Magazine, Entrepreneur Magazine, The CEO Magazine, WSJ Market-Watch, Leader to Leader,* and *Fast Company.*

Chip can be reached at www.chipbell.com.

Contact Chip about his keynotes, webinars, and award-winning training programs.